Masses Nos. 5 and 6

IN FULL SCORE

FRANZ SCHUBERT

From the Critical Edition of 1884–1897

DOVER PUBLICATIONS, INC.
NEW YORK

Copyright

Published in Canada by General Publishing Company, Ltd., 30 Lesmill Road, Don Mills, Toronto, Ontario.
Published in the United Kingdom by Constable and Company, Ltd., 3 The Lanchesters, 162–164 Fulham Palace Road, London W6 9ER.

Bibliographical Note

This Dover edition, first published in 1995, is a new compilation of two works originally published by Breitkopf & Härtel, Leipzig, 1884–1897, in "Serie 13 / Messen / Partitur / Zweiter Band" of *Franz Schubert's Werke / Kritisch durchgesehene Gesammtausgabe*: *Messe (in As) für vier Singstimmen, Orchester und Orgel / Serie 13, No. 5*, and *Messe (in Es) für vier Singstimmen und Orchester . . . Serie 13, No. 6.*

The Dover edition adds: lists of contents and instrumentation; and English translations of the Mass texts, excerpts of critical notes to Mass No. 5 and of headings to that work's two supplements.

Library of Congress Cataloging-in-Publication Data

Schubert, Franz, 1797–1828.
[Masses, D. 678, A♭ major]
Masses nos. 5 and 6 : in full score, from the critical edition of 1884–1897 / Franz Schubert.
1 score.
For soloists (SATB), chorus (SATB), and orchestra.
Latin words.
Reprint. Originally published in: Franz Schubert's Werke. Ser. 13, Messen, edited by Eusebius Mandyczewski. Leipzig : Breitkopf & Härtel, 1884–1897. With new English translations of the Latin words and excerpts from the editorial commentary.
Contents: Mass no. 5 in A-flat major, D. 678 – Mass no. 6 in E-flat major, D. 950.
ISBN 0-486-28832-3 (pbk.)
1. Masses—Scores. I. Mandyczewski, Eusebius. II. Schubert, Franz, 1797–1828. Masses, D. 950, E♭ major.
M2010.S377 D. 678 1995 95-24550
CIP
M

Manufactured in the United States of America
Dover Publications, Inc., 31 East 2nd Street, Mineola, N.Y. 11501

CONTENTS

*A fifth soloist, Tenor II, appears briefly, beginning at p. 237 ("Et incarnatus est").

TEXTS AND TRANSLATIONS

[Bracketed text is omitted in these settings.]

KYRIE

KYRIE eleison. Christe eleison. Kyrie eleison.

GLORIA

GLORIA in excelsis Deo, et in terra pax hominibus bonae voluntatis. Laudamus te, benedicimus te, adoramus te, glorificamus te.

GRATIAS agimus tibi propter magnam gloriam tuam. Domine Deus, Rex coelestis, Deus Pater omnipotens. Domine Fili unigenite, Jesu Christe, Domine Deus, agnus Dei[, Filius Patris.] qui tollis peccata mundi, miserere nobis, Filius Patris, agnus Dei qui tollis peccata mundi, [suscipe deprecationem nostram, qui sedes ad dexteram Patris,] miserere nobis. Quoniam tu solus sanctus, tu solus Dominus, tu solus altissimus. [Jesu Christe,] Cum sancto Spiritu, in gloria Dei Patris, amen.

CREDO

CREDO in unum Deum, [Patrem omnipotentem,] factorem coeli et terrae, visibilium omnium et invisibilium. Et in unum Dominum Jesum Christum, Filium Dei unigenitum, et ex Patre natum ante omnia saecula. Deum de Deo, lumen de lumine, Deum verum de Deo vero, [genitum, non factum, consubstantialem Patri,] per quem omnia facta sunt, qui propter nos homines et propter nostram salutem descendit de coelis.

ET INCARNATUS est de Spiritu sancto ex Maria virgine, et homo factus est. Crucifixus etiam pro nobis sub Pontio Pilato, passus et sepultus est.

ET RESURREXIT tertia die, secundum scripturas, et ascendit in coelum, sedet ad dexteram Patris, et iterum venturus est cum gloria judicare vivos et mortuos, cujus regni non erit finis. Credo in Spiritum sanctum, Dominum et vivificantem, qui ex Patre Filioque procedit, qui cum Patre et Filio simul adoratur et conglorificatur, qui locutus est per Prophetas. [Credo in unam sanctam catholicam et apostolicam ecclesiam,] Confiteor unum baptisma in remissionem peccatorum [et expecto resurrectionem] mortuorum, et vitam venturi saeculi, amen.

SANCTUS

SANCTUS, sanctus, sanctus, Dominus Deus Sabaoth. Pleni sunt coeli et terra gloria tua!
OSANNA in excelsis.

BENEDICTUS

BENEDICTUS qui venit in nomine Domini.
OSANNA in excelsis.

AGNUS DEI

AGNUS DEI qui tollis peccata mundi, miserere nobis.
Agnus Dei qui tollis peccata mundi, miserere nobis.
Agnus Dei qui tollis peccata mundi, dona nobis pacem.

KYRIE

Lord, have mercy on us. Christ, have mercy on us. Lord, have mercy on us.

GLORIA

Glory to God in the highest, and on earth peace to men of good will. We praise thee, we bless thee, we adore thee, we glorify thee.

We give thee thanks for thy great glory. Lord God, heavenly King, God the Father almighty. Lord, the only-begotten Son, Jesus Christ, Lord God, lamb of God, [Son of the Father.] thou who takest away the sins of the world, have mercy on us, Son of the Father, who takest away the sins of the world, [receive our prayer, thou who sittest at the right hand of the Father,] have mercy on us. For thou alone art holy, thou alone art the Lord, thou alone, [Jesus Christ,] with the Holy Ghost, art most high in the glory of God the Father, amen.

CREDO

I believe in one God, [the Father almighty,] maker of heaven and earth, and of all things visible and invisible. And in one Lord Jesus Christ, the only-begotten Son of God, born of the Father before all ages. God of God, light of light, true God of true God, [begotten, not made, consubstantial with the Father,] by whom all things were made, who for us men and for our salvation came down from heaven.

And was incarnate by the Holy Ghost of the Virgin Mary, and was made man. He was crucified also for us under Pontius Pilate, suffered and was buried.

And on the third day He rose again, according to the scriptures, and ascended into heaven, and sitteth at the right hand of the Father, and He shall come again with glory to judge the living and the dead, and His kingdom shall have no end. I believe in the Holy Ghost, the Lord and giver of life, who proceedeth from the Father and the Son, who together with the Father and the Son is worshiped and glorified, who hath spoken by the Prophets. [I believe in one holy catholic and apostolic church,] I confess one baptism for the remission of sins, [and I await the resurrection] of the dead, and the life of the world to come, amen.

SANCTUS

Holy, holy, holy, Lord God of Hosts. Heaven and earth are full of thy glory!
Hosanna in the highest.

BENEDICTUS

Blessed is He that cometh in the name of the Lord.
Hosanna in the highest.

AGNUS DEI

Lamb of God, who takest away the sins of the world, have mercy on us.
Lamb of God, who takest away the sins of the world, have mercy on us.
Lamb of God, who takest away the sins of the world, grant us peace.

NOTES

The following remarks are newly translated excerpts from "Editors' Commentary on the Critical Edition" [*Revisionsbericht*, 1897]—Volume 19 of Dover Publications' *Franz Schubert, Complete Works,* a republication of the Breitkopf & Härtel Critical Edition of 1884–1897. Eusebius Mandyczewski edited the Masses.

MASS NO. 5: SOURCES FOR THIS EDITION

There are four sources for this 1887 Breitkopf & Härtel edition of Mass No. 5:

(1) the full autograph manuscript, marked with the completion date "Sept. 1822";

(2) "a very carefully prepared and beautifully calligraphed copy by Ferdinand Schubert [Franz's older brother] based on the original form of the Mass . . .";

(3) a manuscript organ part of the whole Mass and a manuscript score of the second version of "Hosanna";

(4) the first edition of the work, 1875.

The full autograph manuscript still shows clearly the original form that is revealed by Ferdinand's copy but is full of revisions, which the Breitkopf & Härtel editors adopted.

NOTES TO THE SUPPLEMENTS

Supplement I: Cum sancto Spiritu [p. 143]

The "Cum sancto Spiritu" that begins with measure 7 of page 46 is written in the autograph manuscript on music paper that differs from the paper used for the rest of the Mass. It seems to have been written specially for the revision, because, like all the corrections made in connection with that undertaking, it is characterized by much paler writing. Probably this place was originally occupied by the "Cum sancto Spiritu" that ends the *Gloria* in Ferdinand's copy [see above] and was also engraved in the first printed edition. We include that version in the Supplement.

Supplement II: Second Version of the Hosanna [p. 163]

In a later version Schubert notated the "Hosanna" in common time. The autograph manuscript of this composition has no connection with the autograph manuscript of the entire Mass. Therefore we include this second version of the "Hosanna" in the Supplement.

Mass No. 5 in A-flat Major (D678)
INSTRUMENTATION

Flute [Flauto]
2 Oboes [Oboi]
2 Clarinets in C, A, B♭ [Clarinetti (C, A, B)]
2 Bassoons [Fagotti]

2 Trumpets in C, E, B♭ [Trombe (C, E, B)]
2 Horns in C, E♭, E, F [Corni (C, Es, E, F)]
3 Trombones [Tromboni]

Timpani [Timpani]

Violins I, II [Violino]
Violas [Viola]

Solo Vocal Quartet (SATB)
Full Chorus (SATB)

{ Cellos [Violoncelli/o, Vcl.]
Basses [Basso]
Organ [Organo] }

Mass No. 6 in E-flat Major (D950)
INSTRUMENTATION

2 Oboes [Oboi]
2 Clarinets in B♭ [Clarinetti (B)]
2 Bassoons [Fagotti]

2 Trumpets in C, B♭ [Trombe (C, B)]
2 Horns in E♭, B♭ [Corni (Es, B)]
3 Trombones [Tromboni]

Timpani [Timpani]

Violins I, II [Violino]
Violas [Viola]

Solo Vocal Quartet* (SATB)
Full Chorus (SATB)

Cellos [Violoncello]
Basses [Basso]

*A fifth soloist, Tenor II, appears briefly, beginning at p. 237 ("Et incarnatus est").

Masses Nos. 5 and 6

Mass No. 5 in A-flat Major (D678)

For solo vocal quartet, chorus and orchestra with organ

[Composed 1819–22. 1st edition published 1875; 2nd edition, 1887.]

Kyrie.

November 1819.

lei - son, e - le - i - son, Ky - ri - e — e - lei -
e - lei - son,
Ky - ri - e e - lei - son, e - lei - son, Ky - ri - e, Ky - ri - e — e - lei -
Ky - ri - e e - lei - son, e - lei - son, Ky - ri - e, Ky - ri - e — e - lei -
son, Ky - ri - e — e - lei - son, e - lei - son,
Ky - ri - e e - le - i - son,
son, Ky - ri - e e - le - i - son, e - lei - son,
son,
Vcl.

pp
Solo
Ky-ri-e e-lei- - son.
Christe e-lei-son, Chri-ste, Christe e-lei-
pp
pp
Ky-ri-e e-lei- - son.
pp
fp
fp
fp
fp
fp
fp
pp
pp
pp
p
p
p
p
p
son, Christe e-lei- - son,
Chri-ste e-lei- - son,
e-lei-
Tutti
Solo
Christe e-lei-son,
Chri-ste e-lei - son,
Tutti
Solo
Christe e-lei- - son, Chri-ste, Chri-ste e-lei-son, e-lei- - son, Christe, Christe e-lei-
Tutti
Solo
Christe e-lei- - son,
Chri-ste e-lei- son,
Tutti
Tutti

Solo
Tutti
son, Christe, Christe e_lei_ _ son.
Ky_ri_e_ e_lei_ _
son, e_lei_ _ son.
son, e_lei_ son,
Ky_ri_e e_lei_
Ky_ri_e,
Ky_ri_e e_lei_son, e_lei_ son, Ky_ri_e,
Ky_ri_e_ e_lei_
Ky_ri_e e_lei_son, e_lei_ son,
Ky_ri_e e_lei_
fp
p
pp

son, Ky-ri-e e-lei - son, e-lei - - - - - - son,
Ky-ri-e e-lei-son,
son, Ky-ri-e e-lei - son, e-lei - - - - - son,
son,
Vcl.
pp
Ky-ri-e e-lei - - son.
Solo
Christe e-lei-son, Christe, Christe e-lei - son,
Ky-ri-e e-lei - - son.
Solo
Christe e-
Tutti

Solo
Christe e_lei_son, Chri_ste e_lei_ _son,
Tutti
e_lei_ _son,
Christe e_lei_ _son, Christe e_lei_son, e_lei_ _son,
Tutti
e_lei_ _son,
Solo
Christe
lei_ _son, Christe e_lei_ _son,
Tutti
e_lei_ _son,
Solo
Christe e_lei_ _son, Chri_ste e_lei_ _son, Christe, Chri_ste e_lei_ _son,
Tutti
e_lei_ _son. Ky_ri_e e_lei_ _son, e_lei_
Tutti
Chri_ste
e_lei_ _son. Ky_ri_e e_lei_ _son, e_lei_
pp
cresc.
fp
p
Solo

p
pp
fp
son,
Ky - ri - e e - lei - son, e - lei -
son,
Ky - ri - e e - lei - son, e - lei -
son, e - lei - son, e - lei - son.
son, e - lei - son, e - lei - son.
ppp

Gloria.

Allegro maestoso e vivace.
Flauto.
Oboi.
Clarinetti in A.
Fagotti.
a 2.
Corni in E.
Trombe in E.
3 Tromboni.
Timpani E.H.
Violino I.
Violino II.
Viola.
ff stacc.
Soprano.
Glo - ri - a, glo - ri - a in ex -
Alto.
Tenore
Glo - ri - a, glo - ri - a in ex -
Basso.
Violoncello.
Basso ed Organo.

cel - sis De - - - - - o, glo - ri - a,
cel - sis De - - - - - o, glo - ri - a,

glo - ri - a in ex - cel - - - - - sis et in
glo - ri - a in ex - cel - - - - - sis et in

ter - ra pax ho - mi - nibus bo - nae vo - lun - ta - - tis.
ter - ra pax ho - mi - nibus bo - nae vo - lun - ta - - tis.

fp
ff
p cresc.
cresc.
f
Lau - da - mus te, lau - da - mus
Lau - da - mus te, lau - da - mus

te,
be_ne_di _ ci_mus
te,
glo_
be _
_ ne
_ di _ ci _ mus
te,
te,
be _
_ ne
_ di _
_ ci_mus
te,
glo_
be _
_ ne
_ di _
_ ci_mus
be_ne_di _ ci_mus
te,

ff
f
ri - fi - ca - mus te, glo - ri - fi - ca - mus te,
ri - fi - ca - mus te, glo - ri - fi - ca - mus te,
ad - o -

f
ff
fz
ad - o - ra - mus te.
Glo - ri - fi - ca - mus,
ad - - o - ra - - mus te.
ad - - o - ra - - mus te.
Glo - ri - fi - ca - mus,
ra - - mus, ad - o - ra - mus te.

fz
p
ff
lau - da - mus te,
glo - ri - fi - ca - mus,
lau - da - mus te,
glo - ri - fi - ca - mus,
lau - da - mus te,

p
Solo
ad - o - ra_mus, ad - o - ra - mus te, ad_o - ra - mus te,
ad - o - ra- - - - - - mus te,
ad - o - ra_mus, ad - o - ra- - - - - - mus te,
ad - o - ra - mus, ad - o - ra - mus, ad- - - - o - ra - mus te, ad - o-

cresc.
cresc.
f
ad - o - ra - mus, ad - o - ra - mus te ad - o - ra - mus te,
ad - o ra - - - - - - - mus te,
ad - o - ra - mus, ad - o - ra - - - - - - - mus te,
ra - mus, ad - o - ra - mus, ad - - - - o - ra - mus te,
f
f

ff
a 2.
Tutti
glo - ri - - fi - ca - mus, lau - da - mus te, be - ne - di - ci - mus
glo - ri - - fi - ca - mus, lau - da - mus te, be - ne - di - ci - mus

te,
ad-o-ra - mus te,
lau - da - mus te, glori-fi-ca - mus te, glori-fi-
glo-rifi-camus te, glo-
te,
ad-o-ra - mus te,
lau - da - mus te,
glo-rifi-camus te, glo-

a 2.
ca - mus te.
Glo - ri-a,
ri-fi-camus te.
ri-fi-camus te.
Glo ri-a,

f
fz
glo - ri - a in ex - cel - - sis De - - - - - o,
glo - ri - a in ex - cel - - sis De - - - - - o,

glo - ri_a,
glo - ri_a in ex - cel - - - sis,
glo - ri_a,
glo - ri_a in ex - cel - - - sis,

a 2.
gloria Deo, gloria Deo, gloria De - - o.
gloria Deo, gloria Deo, gloria De - - o.

Andantino.
p
pp
pp
Solo
Gra - ti-as a - gi-mus,

a - gimus ti - bi prop - ter ma - gnam glori - am tu - am, gra - ti - as a - gi - mus
Solo
Gra - ti - as a - gimus ti - bi
Solo
Gra - ti - as a - gi - mus, gra - ti - as a - gi - mus
Solo
p
p

pp
3
pp
pp
pp
Tutti
pp
propter magnam glo - riam tu - am, gra - ti - as a - gi - mus, a - gimus ti - bi,
Tutti
pp
propter — ma - gnam glo - riam tu - am,
Tutti
pp
propter ma - gnam glo - riam tu - am,
a - gimus ti - bi
Tutti pp
prop - ter magnam glo - riam tu - am,
pp
pp

ppp
a 2.
Solo
Tutti
gra_ti_as a_ _gi_mus, a_gimus ti _ bi. Do_mine De_us, Rex coe_le _ stis,
a_gimus ti _ bi. Do_mine De_us, Rex coe_le _ stis,

Solo
gra - ti - as a - gi - mus. De - us Pa - ter, Pa - ter om - ni - po - tens, gra - ti - as
Tutti
tr
gra - ti - as a - gi - mus. De - us Pa - ter, Pa - ter om - ni - po - tens, gra - ti - as

Tutti
Solo
a - gi - mus. Do - mi - ne Je - su Chri - - ste, gra - ti - as a - gimus ti -
gra - ti - as
a - gi - mus. Do - mi - ne Je - su Chri - - ste, gra - ti - as a - gimus ti -
tr
p
pp
f

Tutti
Solo
bi. Fi - li u - ni - ge - ni - te, gra - ti-as a - gimus ti -
gra - ti-as
bi. Fi - li u - ni - ge - ni - te, gra - ti-as a - gimus ti -
pp

a 2.
Tutti
bi. Domine Deus, Rex coelestis, Deus Pater omnipotens.
Tutti
Tutti
bi. Domine Deus, Rex coelestis, Deus Pater omnipotens.
Tutti

Solo
Gra_ti_as a - gi - mus, a - gimus ti - bi propter ma - gnam
Solo
Gra_ti_as a - gi_mus, a _ gimus ti _ bi propter magnam
Solo

gloriam tuam, propter magnam gloriam tuam, gratias agi-
Solo
propter magnam gloriam tuam,
gloriam tuam, propter magnam gloriam tuam,
propter magnam gloriam tuam,

Tutti
pp
Solo
Tutti
ppp
mus, a-gimus ti - bi, gra - ti-as a - gi-mus, a-gimus ti - bi.
a-gimus ti - bi, a-gimus ti - bi.

Allegro moderato.
Solo
Tutti
Domine Deus, agnus Dei qui tollis peccata mundi,
miserere, miserere
miserere, miserere

no - bis,
no - bis,
Solo
Do-mine

pp
fp
Tutti
mi - se-re - re, mi - se-re - re no -
mi - se-re-re, mi - se-re - re no -
De-us, a-gnus De-i qui tol-lis pec-ca - ta mun-di,

bis,
bis,
Solo
Fi - li-us

fp
pp
mi - se-re - re, mi - se-re - re_ no -
Tutti
Pa-tris, a - gnus De - i qui tol - lis pec-ca - - ta mun-di, mi - se-re - re, mi - se-re - re_ no -

a 2.
bis.
Quo - ni-
bis.
Quo - ni-

cresc.
p
f
am tu so - lus san - ctus, tu so - lus al - tis - si
am tu so - lus san - ctus, tu so - lus al - tis - si -

cresc.
ff
fz
mus, tu so - lus Do - mi - nus, tu

a 2.
a 2.
Solo
Tutti
so_lus, so_lus_ sanctus, tu so_lus al_tis_simus, tu so_lus_ Do_minus,
tu so_lus al_
Solo
Tutti
Solo
Tutti
so_lus, so_lus_ sanctus, tu so_lus al_tis_simus, tu so_lus_ Do_minus,
tu so_lus al_
Solo
Tutti

tr
Solo
Tutti
tis_simus,
tu so_lus al_tis_simus, tu,
tu so_
tis_simus,
tu so_lus al_tis_simus, tu,
tu so_

a 2.
lus Do mi nus.
lus Do mi nus.
lus Do mi nus.
lus Do mi nus. Cum sancto Spi ri tu in glo ri a De i Pa tris,

Cum sancto Spi-ri-tu in glo-ri-a De-i Pa-tris, a-
a-men, a-men, a-men, in glo-ri-a De-i Pa-tris, a

a 2.
Cum sancto Spi_ri_tu in
Cum san_cto Spi_ri_tu in glo _ ri_a De _ i Pa _ tris, a _ _ men, a _ _ men,
men. cum san _ cto Spi _ ri _ tu in glo_ri_a De _ _ i Pa _ tris
men, a _ men, a _ men, a_men, a _ _ men,

glo - ri-a De - i Pa - - tris, a - - - - - men, a - - men, a -
a - - men, in glo-ri-a De-i Pa - tris, a - men,cum san-cto Spi-ri-tu in glo-ri-a De-i
a - men, a - men, a - - - - men,cum san-cto Spi-ri - tu in glo-ri-a De-i
cum san-cto Spi - ri-tu in glo - ri-a

men, cum sancto Spi - ri - tu, a - men, a -
Pa - tris, a - men, a - men, a - men, a - men, a - men, a - men, a -
Pa - tris, a - men, a - men, a - men, a - men, a -
De - i Pa - tris, a - men, a - men, a - men, a -

men, a - - men, a - - - - - - - - men, a - - - men, a - - -
men, a - - men, a - - - - - - men, a - - - - - - - - - - - -
men, a - - men, a - - - - men, a - - men, a -
men, a - - men, a - - men, a - - - - - men.

men, a - - - - - men, Pa - - tris,
men, a - - men, cum san - cto Spi - ri - tu in glo - ri - a De - i
- - men, cum sancto Spi - ri - tu in glo - ri - a De - i Pa - tris
a - - - - - - - - men, cum sancto Spi - ri - tu in glo - - ri - a De - i -

a 2.
a - men,
cum sancto Spi - ri-tu in glo-ri-a De - i Pa - tris, a -
cum sancto Spi - ri-tu in glo - ri-a De - i Pa - tris, a - men, a -
a - men, a - men, a - men, a - men.
Pa - tris,
a -

men, a
men, a
men, a
men, a
men, a
men, a
men, a
men, a
men, a
men, a
men, a
men, a

a 2.
a 2.
men, a - - - - - - - men, a - - men, a -
men, cum sancto Spi-ri-tu in glo-ri-a De - i Pa - - tris,
De - i Pa - tris, a - - men, a - men.
men, a-men, a - - - - - - men, a - - men. a -

men, cum sancto Spi-ri-tu in glo-ri-a De-i Pa- - - - - - tris, a-
a - - - - men, cum sancto Spi-ri-tu in glo-ri-a De-i Pa- - - - tris, a- - -
cum, sancto Spi-ri-tu in glo - ri-a De - i Pa- tris, a - men,
- - - - - men, a- men, a - men, a - - - - men,

men, a - - - - - - - - men, a - men, a - - -
men, a - men, a - men, a - - - - - - - men, a - men, a - men, a - -
a - men, a - men, a - men, a - - - - - men, a - men, a - men, a - men,
a - men, a - men, a - men, a - - - - men, a -

- - - - men, a - - men, a - - - men, a - men.
- - - - men, a - men, a - men, a - - - - - men, a - men, a - men,
a - - - - men, a - men, a - men, a - - - - - - - men, a - men,
- - - - - - men, a - - men, a - - men, a - - men, a - - - men, a - - men,

a - men, a - men a - men,
a - men, a - men, cum sancto Spi - ri - tu in glo - ri - a De - i Pa - tris,
a - men, a - men, a - men, a - men, a -
a - men, a - men, a - men, a - men, a - men, a -

cum sancto Spi-ri-tu in glo-ri-a De-i Pa-tris, a-men, a-men,
a-men, a-men, a-men, a-men, a-
-men, a-men, a-men, a-men, a-
-men,
a-men, a-men, a-

a - - - - men, a - - - - - - men, a - - - - - - - - men,
- men, a - - - - - - - - - men, a - men, a - men, a - - -
- - - men, a - men, a - - - - - - - - - - - men, a - men, a - - -
- men, a - - - - men, a - - - men, a - - -

fz
a - - - - - men, a - men.
- men, a - - - men, a - men.
- men, a - - - - - men Cum sancto Spi - ri - tu in glo - ri - a De - i
men, a - - - men, a - men. Cum sancto Spi - ri - tu in glo - ri - a De - i Pa - tris,

Cum sancto Spi-ri-tu in glo-ri-a De-i Pa-tris a-
Cum sancto Spi-ri-tu in glo-ri-a De-i Pa-tris,
Pa-tris, a-men, a-men, a-men, a-men, a-men,
a-men, a-men, a-men, a-men,
a-

- - - - - men, a - - - - - - men,
cum sancto
a - - - - - - - - - - - men,
cum sancto Spi - ri - tu, a - -
a - - - - - - - - - men, cum sancto Spi - ri - tu in glo - ri - a De - - i,
- - - - - - - - - - - men,

Spi-ri-tu in glo-ri-a De-i Pa-tris, a- men,
men, a-men, a- men, a-men, a- men, cum sancto
a- men, a-men, a- men, cum sancto Spi-ri-tu in
cum sancto Spi-ri-tu in glo-ri-a De-i Pa-tris, a-men, a-
fz
fz
fz
fz

cum sancto Spi-ri-tu in glo-ri-a De-i Pa-tris, a-men, cum sancto
Spi-ri-tu in glo-ri-a De-i Pa-tris, a-men,
glo-ri-a De-i Pa-tris, a-men, cum sancto Spi-ri-tu in
men a-

Spi-ri-tu in glo-ri-a De-i Pa-tris, a- - - - - - - - - - - men,
cum sancto Spi-ri-tu in glo-ri-a De- - i Pa- - - tris, a-men a- - -
glo-ri-a De- i Pa- tris, a- - - - - - - - - - - - men,

a - - - men, a - - men, a - - - men, a - men, a - men.
- - - - men, a - - men, a - - - men, a - men, a - men.
a - - - men, a - - men, a - - - men, a - men, a - men.
- - - - men. a - - men, a - - - men, a - men, a - men.

Credo.

Allegro maestoso e vivace.
Oboi.
Clarinetti in C.
Fagotti.
Corni in C.
Trombe in C.
3 Tromboni.
Timpani in C. G.
Violino I.
Violino II.
Viola.
Soprano.
Cre_do in u_num De_um, fa_cto_rem coe_li et ter_ _rae.
Alto.
Tenore.
Cre_do in u_num De_um, fa_cto_rem coe_li et ter_ _rae.
Basso.
Violoncello, Basso ed Organo.

Cre_do in fa_cto_rem coe_li et ter_rae, vi_si_bi_li_um om_ni_um et in_vi_si_bi_li_um.
Cre_do in fa_cto_rem coe_li et ter_rae, vi_si_bi_li_um om_ni_um et in_vi_si_bi_li_um.

a 2.
Cre - do. cre - do in u - num Do - mi - num Je - sum Chri - stum.
Cre - do. cre - do, cre - do in Fi - li - um De -

Cre - do. Et ex Pa-tre na - tum an-te om-ni-a sae-cu - la.
i u-ni-ge-ni - tum.
Cre - do De -
Vcl.
Tutti

Cre - - do De - - um ve - - rum de De - o - ve - ro. Cre - -
um de De - - o, lu - men de lu - mi - ne.
Cre - -

do, per quem om - ni - a fa - cta sunt, per quem om - ni - a fa - cta sunt, qui propter nos ho - mi - nes
do, per quem om - ni - a fa - cta sunt, per quem om - ni - a fa - cta sunt, qui propter nos ho - mi - nes
per quem om - - - ni - a fa - cta sunt, per quem om - - - ni - a

a 2.
et propter nostram sa_lu_tem de_scen_dit de coe_lis, de_scen_dit de coe_lis. Cre_
coe_lis.
et propter nostram sa_lu_tem de_scen_dit de coe_lis, de_scen_dit de coe_lis. Cre_
coe_lis. Cre_

do, per quem om - ni - a fa - cta sunt, per quem om - ni - a fa - cta sunt. Cre - - - - -
do, per quem om - ni - a fa - cta sunt, per quem om - ni - a fa - cta sunt. Cre - - - -
do, per quem om - - ni - a fa - cta sunt, per quem om - - - ni - a

do,
cre - - - - do.
do,
cre - - - - do.
Cre - - - - do.

Grave.
in B.
in Es.
cresc.
Et in-car - na- - - tus est ex Ma-ri-a vir - - - gi-ne, et ho - mo
vir - gi - ne,
Et in-car-na-tus est de Spi-ri - tu san - cto ex Ma-ri-a vir - gi-ne, et ho - mo

fa - ctus est. · Et in-car - na-tus est de Spi-ri-tu san - cto ex Ma-ri - a vir-gi-ne,
fa - ctus est. Et in-car-natus est de Spiri-tu san - cto ex Ma-ri - a vir - gi - ne,
dim.

ppp
cresc.
ff
pp
et ho - mo fa - ctus est. Cru - - ci - fi - xus,
et ho - mo fa - ctus est. Cru - - ci - fi - xus, cru - ci - fi - xus
Cru - ci -

a 2.
a 2.
a 2.
a 2.
a 2.
a 2.
cru - ci - fi - xus e - tiam pro nobis, cru - ci - fi - xus, cru - ci - fi - xus
cru - ci - fi - xus pro nobis, cru - ci - fi - xus, cru - ci - fi - xus e - tiam pro
e - tiam pro no - bis, pro — no - bis, cru - ci - fi - xus,
fi - xus e - ti - am pro no - bis, cru - ci - fi - xus, cru - ci -

pp
pp
pp
pp
pp
pp
pp
dim.
dim.
dim.
e - ti_am pro no - - - bis cru - ci - fi_xus e - tiam pro no_bis, sub Pon - ti_o Pi - la - to pas - sus
pp
no - bis, pro no - - bis,
pp
cru - ci - fi - xus pro nobis, cru - ci - fi_xus e - tiam pro no_bis, sub Pon - ti_o Pi - la - to pas - sus
pp
fi - xus e - tiampro nobis,
pp
dim.

Tempo I.
ppp
pp
in C.
in C.
f
p
et se - pul - - - tus est.
Et re - sur - re - xit
et se - pul - - - tus est.
Et re - sur - re - xit

p
cresc.
p cresc.
p
cresc.
p cresc.
p cresc.
cresc.
poco
a
poco
cresc.
poco
a
poco
cresc.
poco
a
poco
cresc.
poco
a
poco
ter - ti - a di - - e se - cun - - dum scrip - tu - - ras, et a - scen -
cresc.
poco
a
poco
cresc.
poco
a
poco
ter - ti - a di - - e se - cun - - dum scrip - tu - - ras, et a - scen -
cresc.
poco
a
poco
cresc.
poco
a
poco

cresc.
a 2.
dit in coe - lum, se - det ad dex - te-ram Pa - tris, se -
dit in coe - lum, se - det ad dex - te-ram Pa - tris, se -

fz
a 2.
det, se - - det ad dex_teram Pa - tris, se - - det,
det, se - - det ad dex_teram Pa - tris, se - - det,

a 2.
a 2.
a 2.
a 2.
a 2.
se - - det ad dex-te-ram Pa - tris, et i - te-rum ven - tu - rus est cum glo-ri-a, ju-di-
se - - det ad dex-te-ram Pa - tris, et i - te-rum ven - tu - rus est cum glo-ri-a, ju-di-

ca_re vi_vos et mor_ _ _ _tu_os, cu_jus re_gni non e_rit fi_ _ _ _ _ _
ca_re vi_vos et mor_ _ _ _tu_os, cu_jus re_gni non e_rit fi_ _ _ _ _ _

a 2.
ff
f
fz
cresc.
nis. Cre - do, cre - do in Spi - ri-tum san -
Spi - ri-tum san - ctum Do - mi-
nis. Cre - do, cre - do Spi - ri-tum san - ctum Do - mi-
cre - do, cre - do, cre -

ctum. san - - - ctum Do - mi - num. Cre - - - do, cre - - -
num. Spi - ri - tum san - ctum
num. Spi ri tum san ctum Do - mi - num. Cre - - - do. cre - - -
do, cre - - - do. cre - - - do.

do et vi - vi - - fi - can - - - - - -
et vi - vi - fi - can - - tem, et vi - vi - fi - can - -
do et vi - vi - fi - can - - tem, et vi - vi - fi - can - -
et vi - vi - - fi - can - - tem, et vi - vi - - fi - can - -

tem. Cre - do, cre - do, qui ex Pa -
tem. Cre - do, cre - do, qui ex Pa -
tem. Cre - do, cre - do, qui ex Pa
tem. Cre - do, cre - do, cre - do, cre -

a 2.
ff
ffz
f
tre Fi - li - o - que pro - ce - - dit. Cre - - do, cre -
tre Fi - li - o - que pro - ce - - dit. Cre - - do, cre -
tre Fi - - li - o - que pro - ce - - dit. Cre - - do, cre -
do, cre - - do, cre - - do. Cre - - do, cre -

do, qui cum Pa_tre et Fi_ _ _ _li_o si_ _ _mul ad_o_ra_ _
do, qui cum_ Pa_tre et Fi_li _ o si_ _ mul ad_ o_ ra_ _
do, qui cum_ Pa_tre et Fi_li _ o si_ _ mul ad_ o_ ra_ _
do, qui cum_ Pa_tre et Fi_li _ o si_ _ mul ad_ _o_ra_ _

tur, qui cum Pa - tre et Fi - - li - o con - glo - ri - fi - ca - - -
tur, qui cum Pa - tre et Fi - - li - o con - glo - ri - fi - ca - -

fz
fz
fz
fz decresc.
f
p
tur, qui lo - cu - tus est per Pro - phe - - tas.
tur, qui lo - cu - tus est per Pro - phe - - tas.
fz decresc.

Con-fi - te-or u - - - num bap - tis - - - - - ma
Con-fi - te-or u - - - num bap - tis - - - - - ma
Violoncelli
mf staccato

fp
in re_mis_si - o - - nem pec_ca - to - rum mortu - o - - - rum.
in re_mis_si - o - - nem pec_ca - to - rum mortu - o - - - rum.

Et vi- -tam ven- -tu- -ri sae- -cu- li,
Et vi- -tam ven- -tu- -ri sae- -cu- li,
Tutti

vi- - tam ven- tu- - ri sae- cu- li.
vi- - tam ven- tu- - ri sae- cu- li.

A - - - - - - - - - - - - - men,
A - - - - - - - - - - - - - men,

a- - - - - - - - - - - - - - - -men,
a- - - - - - - - - - - - - - - - -men,

a 2.
Solo
a - - - - men, a - - - - men, a - - - - - - - - - men, a - men, a - men,
Tutti
Solo
Tutti
Solo
a - - - - men, a - - - - men, a - - - - - - - - - men, a - men, a - men,
Tutti
Solo
Tutti

a – men, a – men, a – men, a – – – – – – – – men, a – men, a – men.
a – men, a – men, a – men, a – – – – – – – – men, a – men, a – men,

fp
a 2.
ff
Solo
Tutti
a - men, a - men, a - men, a - men, a - - - - - - - - men, a - men, a - men,
a - men, a - men, a - men, a - men, a - - - - - - - - men, a - men, a - men,

a - men, a - men, a - men, a - - - - - - - - men, a - - men,
a - men, a - men, a - men, a - - - - - - - - men, a - - men,

cresc.
cresc.
cresc.
cresc.
cresc.
cresc.
cresc.
cresc.
cresc.
cresc.
cresc.
a - - - - - men, a - men.
a - - - - - - - - - - men, a - men.

Sanctus.

Andante.
Flauto.
Oboi.
Clarinetti in C.
Fagotti.
Corni in F.
Trombe in B.
3 Tromboni.
Timpani in F.C.
Violino I.
Violino II.
Viola.
Soprano.
Alto.
Tenore.
Basso.
Violoncello, Basso ed Organo.
San- - - -ctus,
San- - - -ctus.

pp
cresc.
ff
fp decresc.
p
p cresc.
San- - -ctus,

pp
cresc.
ff
a 2.
p cresc.
San- - - -ctus Do- -mi- nus De- -us
San- - - -ctus Do mi nus De- us

ffz
decresc.
p
3 3 3
Sa - - - ba - oth. Ple - - ni sunt coe li et ter - -
Sa - - - ba - oth. Ple - - ni sunt coe li et ter - -

p
p
p
ra,
ple - - ni sunt coe - li et ter - -
ra,
ple - - ni sunt coe - li et ter - -

ra,
ple- - ni sunt coe- li et ter- -
ra,
ple- - ni sunt coe- li et ter- -

p
ra,
ple - - - ni sunt glo - ri - a tu - - -
ra,
ple - - - ni sunt glo - ri - a tu - - -

decresc.

decresc.

pp

pp

decresc.

pp

a, glo - ri - a tu - - a.

pp

pp

a, glo - ri - a tu - - a.

pp

decresc.

Allegro.
fp
p
cresc.
O-san-na in excelsis De-o, o-san-na, o-san-na,
o-san-na in ex-
O-san-na, o-san-na, o-san-na, o-san-na in ex-

o-san-
-na,
o-san-na, o-san-na,
o-san-na,
cel-sis De-
-o,
o-san-na
cel-sis De-
-o,
o-san-na in excelsis De-o,
o-san-na,
o-san-na, o-san-na
o-san-
-na.
cresc.

cresc.
cresc.
cresc.
cresc.
a 2.
o-san-na, o-san-na, o-san-na.
in excel-sis De-o,
in excel-sis De-o, o-san-na, o-san-na.
in excel-sis De-o,
cresc.

Benedictus.

Andante con moto.
Flauto.
Oboi.
Fagotti.
Corni in Es.
Violino I.
Violino II.
Viola.
Soprano.
Alto.
Tenore.
Basso.
Violoncello, Basso ed Organo.
pizz.
Solo
Be - ne - di - ctus qui ve - nit in
Solo
Solo
Be - ne - di - ctus qui ve - nit in
no - - - - mi - ne Do - mi - - ni, be - ne - di - ctus qui ve - - nit in
no - - - mi - ne Do - mi - ni, be - ne - di - ctus qui ve - - nit in

a 2.
a 2.
Tutti
no - mi-ne Do - mi-ni.
Be - ne - di - ctus qui ve - nit in
Tutti
Tutti
no - mi-ne Do - mi-ni.
Be - ne - di - ctus qui ve - nit in
arco
no - mi-ne Do - mi - ni.
Solo
Bene-di - ctus qui ve - nit
Solo
Be - ne - di-ctus qui ve - nit
Solo
no - mi-ne Do - mi - ni.
Be - ne - di-ctus qui ve - nit

Solo
Bene_di_ctus qui ve_
Tutti
in no_mi_ne Do_mi_ni, be_ne_di_ctus qui ve_nit,
Solo
Bene_di_ctus qui ve_
Tutti
in_ no_mi_ne Do_mi_ni, be_ne_di_ctus qui ve_nit,
Solo
Bene_di_ctus qui ve_
Tutti
in_ no_mi_ne Do_mi_ni, be_ne_di_ctus qui ve_nit,
a 2.
cresc.
nit,
Tutti
qui ve_nit in no_mi_ne Do_mi_ni.
nit,
Tutti
nit,
Tutti
qui ve_nit in no_mi_ne Do_mi_ni.
qui ve_nit in

Solo
Be - ne- -di - ctus qui ve - nit in no- - -mi - ne Do - mi -
Solo
Solo
Be - ne- -di - ctus qui ve - nit in no- - -mi - ne Do - mi-
pizz.
pp
pp
pp
pp
ni, be - ne - di - ctus qui ve- -nit in no- - -mi - ne Do- -mi-
ni, be - ne - di - ctus qui ve- -nit in no- - -mi - ne Do- -mi-

a 2.
Tutti
ni, be- ne- -di- ctus qui ve- -nit in no- - - -mi- ne Do- mi-
Tutti
Tutti
ni, be- ne- -di- ctus qui ve- -nit in no- - - -mi- ne Do- mi-
arco
p Solo
ni, be- ne- -di- ctus qui ve- -nit in no- - -mi- ne Do- mi-
p Solo
bene- di- ctus qui ve- nit in no- mi- ne Do- mi-
p Solo
ni, be- ne- -di- ctus qui ve- -nit in no- - -mi- ne Do- mi-

Solo
bene-di - - ctus qui ve - - nit in no - - - mi-ne
Tutti
ni. bene-di - - ctus qui ve - - nit in no-mine Do-mi-ni,
Solo bene-di - - ctus qui ve - - nit in no - - - - - mi-ne
Tutti
bene-di - - ctus qui ve - - nit in no-mine Do-mi-ni,
Solo bene-di - - ctus qui ve - - nit in no - - - - - mi-ne
Tutti
ni. bene-di - - ctus qui ve - - nit in no-mine Do-mi-ni,
p
Do - mi - ni, bene-di - - ctus qui ve-nit in no - - - mi-ne Do - - - - - -
bene-di - - ctus qui ve - - nit,
Do - mi - ni, bene-di - - ctus qui ve-nit in no - - - mi-ne Do - - - - - -
bene-di - - ctus qui ve - - nit,
Do - mi - ni, bene-di - - ctus qui ve-nit in no - - - mi-ne Do - - - - - -
bene-di - - ctus qui ve - - nit,
a 2.
cresc.

cresc.
mi- ni.
Tutti bene-di- ctus qui ve- nit in no- mi-ne Do-
decresc.
mi- ni.
Segue Osanna.
Pag. 118.

Agnus Dei.

Adagio.
Flauto.
Oboi.
Clarinetti in B.
Fagotti.
Corni in Es.
Trombe in B.
3 Tromboni.
Timpani in F. C.
Violino I.
con sordino
Violino II.
con sordino
Viola.
con sordino
Soprano.
Solo
A_ _gnus De_ _i
Alto.
Solo
A_ _gnus
Tenore.
Solo
A_ _gnus
Basso.
Violoncello, Basso ed Organo.

Tutti
a_gnus De_i qui tol_lis pec_ca_ta, pec_ca_ _ _ta_ mun_ _ _ _ _di, mi_se_
Tutti
De_ _ _ _i
Tutti
De_ _ _ _i qui tol_lis pec_ca_ta, pec_ca_ _ _ _ta_ mun_ _ _ _ _di, mi_se_
Solo
Tutti
A_gnus De_ _i qui
Vcl.

re- -re, mi-se-re- -re no- - - - - -bis.
re- -re, mi- se- re- -re no- - - - - -bis.
Tutti

Solo
A - gnus De - - - i qui tol - lis pec - ca - ta, pec - ca -
Solo
Solo
A - gnus De - i, a - gnus De - i qui tol - lis pec - ca - ta, pec - ca -
Solo
A - gnus De - i qui
pp
p

Tutti
-ta mun - - - - -di, mi-se-re- -re, mi-se-re- -re no- - - -
Tutti
Tutti
-ta mun - - - - -di, mi-se-re- -re, mi-se-re- -re no- - - -
Tutti
Vcl.
Tutti

Solo
bis.
A - gnus De - i, a - gnus De - i,
Solo
A - gnus De - - - - i,
Solo
bis.
A - gnus De - - - - i,
Solo
A - gnus De - i,

Allegretto.
senza sordino
senza sordino
senza sordino
Tutti
Solo
a-gnus, a-gnus De - - - - - -i. Do-na no-bis pa- -cem, do-na
Tutti
Solo
Tutti
Solo
a-gnus, a-gnus De - - - - - -i. Do-na no-bis pa- -cem, do-na
Tutti
Vcl.

p
p
p
ff
a 2.
ff Tutti
no-bis pa- -cem, do-na no-bis pa- -cem, do-na no-bis pa- -cem, do-na
ff Tutti
ff Tutti
no-bis pa- -cem, do-na no-bis pa- -cem, do-na no-bis pa- -cem, do-na
Tutti
f
ff

Solo
Tutti
no_bis pa_cem, do_na no_bis pa_cem, do_na no_bis pa_cem. Do_na no_bis pa_
Solo
Tutti
Solo
Tutti
no_bis pa_cem, do_na no_bis pa_cem, do_na no_bis pa_cem. Do_na no_bis pa_
Vcl.
decresc.
Tutti
a 2.

Solo
Tutti
Solo
Tutti
cem, do-na no-bis pa- -cem, do-na no-bis pacem, pacem, do-na no-bis pa-cem,
Solo
Tutti
Solo
Tutti
Solo
Tutti
Solo
Tutti
cem, do-na no-bis pa- -cem, do-na— no-bis pacem, pacem, do-na— no-bis pa-cem,
Tutti

pacem, do - na no - bis pa - - cem, do - na no - bis, nobis pa - cem. Do - na
pacem, do - na no - bis pa - - cem, do - na no - bis, nobis pa cem. Do na
pa - - cem,
Solo
Tutti
Vcl.
cresc.

139
p
ff
a 2.
ff Tutti
no - bis pa - - cem, do - na no - bis pa - - cem, do - na no - bis
do - na no - bis
no - bis pa - - cem, do - na no - bis pa - - cem, do - na no - bis
Tutti

Solo
pa_ _cem, do_na no_ _bis pa_ _ _cem,
Tutti
do_na nobis pa_ _cem,
Solo
do_na
Solo
Tutti
Solo
Solo
pa_ _cem, do_na no_ _bis pa_ _ _cem,
Tutti
do_na nobis pa_ _cem,
Solo
do na
Vcl.
Tutti
Vcl.

Tutti

Solo

no- bis pa- cem, do- na no- bis- pa- - - cem, do- na no- bis pa- - - -

Tutti

Solo

Tutti

Solo

no- bis pa- - cem, do- na no- bis- pa- - - - cem, do- na no- bis pa- - - -

Solo

Tutti

(September 1822.)

SUPPLEMENT I.

Cum sancto Spiritu.

fz
Cum sancto Spi - ritu in glo - ri - a De - - i, in glo - ri - a Pa - tris, a - - -
men. Cum sancto Spi - ritu in glo - ri - a Pa - tris, a - -

men, a - - men, cum sancto
men. Cum sancto Spi - ritu in glo - ri - a De - i, in glo - ri - a Pa - tris, a - - -
Cum sancto Spi - ritu in glo - ri - a De - i, in glo - ri - a Pa - tris, a - - -

fz
div.
f
Cum sancto Spi - ritu in glo - ri - a De - i, in glo - ri - a Pa - tris, a -
men.
men, a - men. Cum sancto Spi - ritu in glo - ri - a De - i, in glo - ri - a Pa - tris, a -
Vel.

ff
a 2.
Tutti
men, cum sancto Spi-ritu in glo-ri-a De-i, in glo-ri-a Pa-tris, a- -men,
men, a-men,
men, a-men, cum sancto Spi-ritu in glo-ri-a De-i, in glo-ri-a Pa-tris, a- -men,

p
cum sancto Spi-ritu in glo-ri-a De-i, in glo-ri-a Pa-tris, a-men, cum sancto
cum sancto Spi-ritu in glo-ri-a De-i, in glo-ri-a Pa-tris, a-men, cum sancto
Vcl.

a 2.
a 2.
Spi - ritu in glo - ri - a De - i, cum sancto Spi - ritu in glo - ri - a Pa - tris,
in glo - ri - a
Spi - ritu in glo - ri - a De - i, cum sancto Spi - ritu in glo - ri - a Pa - tris, in
in glo - ri - a De - -
Tutti
Vel.
Tutti

in glo - ri - a De - i Pa - tris, in glo - ri - a De - i, in
De - i Pa - tris, De - i Pa - tris, in glo - ri - a De - i, in
glo - ri - a, glo - ri - a De - i Pa - tris, in glo - ri - a
- i Pa - tris, in

decresc.
p
decresc.
p
p
glo - ri - a De - i Pa - - tris, cum sancto Spi - ritu in glo - ri - a De - i, in glo - ri - a
p
p
De - - - - i Pa - - - - tris, cum sancto Spi - ritu in glo - ri - a De - i, in glo - ri - a
glo - ri - a De - - i Pa - - - tris,
Vcl.
p

a 2.
a 2.
Pa - tris, a - - men,
in glo - ri - a Pa - tris, a - - men,
Pa - tris, a - - men,
in glo - ri - a Pa - tris, a - - men,
in glo - ri - a De - i Pa - - tris, a - - men, in
Tutti

a 2.
in glo - ri - a Pa - tris, a - - men, in
cum san - cto Spi - ri - tu
in glo - ri - a Pa - tris, a - - men, cum san - cto Spi - ri - tu in
glo - ri - a De - i Pa - - tris,
Vel.

a 2.
Tutti
glo - ri_a De - i, cum san - cto Spi - ritu in glo - ri_a Pa - tris, a - - men,
glo - ri_a De - i, cum san - cto_ Spi_ri_tu a - -
in glo - ri_a Pa - tris,

fz
a - - - men, a - - - men, a - - - men, a - men, a - men,
men, a - - - men, a - - - men, a - - - men, a - men,

a - men a - men, a- - - men, cum sancto Spi - ritu in
cum sancto Spi - ritu in glo - ri - a De - i, in
a - men, a - men, a- - - men, cum sancto Spi - ritu in glo - ri - a De - i, in
a - men, cum sancto spi - ritu in glo - - - - - - - - - - -

cresc.
cresc.
cresc.
cresc.
cresc.
cresc.
cresc.
cresc.
cresc.
cresc.
glo - ri - a De - i, cum sancto Spi - ritu in glo - ri - a De - i, in glo - ri - a Pa - tris, a -
glo - ri - a Pa - tris, a - men, cum sancto Spi - ritu in glo - ri - a De - i Pa - tris, a
glo - ri - a Pa - tris, a - men, cum sancto Spi - ritu in glo - ri - a De - i Pa - tris, a -
- ri - a
cresc.

ben marcato

ben marcato

- men, cum sancto Spi-ritu in glo-ri-a De-i, in glo-ri-a Patris, a - men, cum san-cto Spi - ritu in

men,

men, cum sancto Spi-ritu in glo-ri-a De-i, in glo-ri-a Patris, a - men, cum san-cto Spi - ritu in

- men,

ff ben marcato

fz
p
a 2.
glo - ri - a De - i, in glo - ri - a Pa - tris, a - - - men, cum san - cto Spi - ritu in
glo - ri - a De - i, in glo - ri - a Pa - tris, a - - - men, cum san - cto Spi - ritu in

cresc.
ff
fz
a2.
glo - ri - a De - i, in glo - ri - a Pa - tris, a - men, in glo - ri - a Pa - tris, a -
glo - ri - a De - i, in glo - ri - a Pa - tris, a - men, in glo - ri - a Pa - tris, a -

a 2.
fz
p
men, in glo - - - - ri - a De - - i Pa - - tris,
men, in glo - - - - ri - a De - - i Pa - - tris,

Tutti
a - men,
a - men.
a - men,
a - men.

SUPPLEMENT II.

Second Version of the Hosanna.

a 2.
p
cresc.
ff
fz
fp
san - na,
o - san - - - na!
O
o - san - - na in ex - celsis De - - - o!
O - san - na in excel - sis
O - san - - - - na!

a 2.
p cresc.
fp
fz f
san - na, o - san - na, o - san - na,
o
o - san - na in ex - cel - sis
De - o, o - san - na, o - san - na, o - san - na in ex - cel - sis

a 2.
san - na, o - san - na, o - san - na!
De - o,
De - o, o - san - na, o - san - na!

Mass No. 6 in E-flat Major (D950)

For solo vocal quartet, chorus and orchestra

[Composition begun June 1828. Published 1865.]

Kyrie.

pp
pp
pp
pp
pp
pp
pp
fp
pp
fp
pp
fp
pp
fp
Ky - ri - e. Ky - ri - e e - lei - - son, e - lei - -
pp
fp
pp
fp
Ky - ri - e. Ky - ri - e e - lei - son, e - lei - -
pp
fp
pp
fp
pp
fp

son,
Ky - ri - e — e - le - - - i - son,
e - le - - i - - son,
son,
Ky - ri - e e - le - - - i - son,

a 2.
div.
fp
Ky - ri - e — e - le - - i - son, Ky - ri - e e - lei -
e - lei - son,
Ky - ri - e e - lei - - son, Ky - ri - e e - lei -
e - lei - son,

a 2.
son, e - lei - son, Ky - ri - e e - lei - - son, e - lei - - - - - -
son, e - lei - son, Ky - ri - e e - lei - - son, e - lei - - - - - -

cresc.
f
ff
son!
Chri - ste e - lei - son, e - lei - - son,
son!
Chri - ste e - lei - son, e - lei - - son,

a 2.
cresc.
f
ff
p
Chri - ste e - lei - son, e - lei - - - son.
Chri ste e lei son, e - lei - - - son.

decresc.
p
Chri - ste, Christe e - lei - son, e - lei - son, e - lei - son!
e - lei - son,
pp
Chri - ste, e - lei - son, e -

pp
decresc.
Ky - ri - e, Ky - ri - e e - lei - - son, e -
fp
lei - son, e - lei - son! Ky - ri - e, Ky - ri - e e - lei - son, e -

lei - son.
Ky ri - e — e - lei
lei - son.
Ky - ri - e e - lei

son. Ky - ri - e — e - lei - - on. Ky - ri-e e -
son. Ky - ri - e e - lei - - son. Ky - ri-e e -

fp
pp
a 2.
lei - son, e - lei - son, Ky - ri - e e - lei - son, e - lei - - -
lei - son, e - lei - son, Ky - ri - e e - lei - son, e - lei - - -

ff
decresc.
son,
Kyrie, Kyrie e-
p
div.
pizz.
arco

p
cresc.
lei

p
pp
decresc.
pizz.
-son, e - lei - - - - son,
Ky - ri - e
son.
son, e - lei - - - - son,
Ky - ri - e
- son.

ff
p
pp
arco
Ky - ri - e e - lei - - - son, e - lei - son!
Ky - ri - e e - lei - - - son, e - lei - son!

Gloria.

Allegro moderato e maestoso.
Oboi.
Clarinetti in B.
Fagotti.
Corni in B.
Trombe in B.
3 Tromboni.
Timpani in B. F.
Violino I.
Violino II.
Viola.
Soprano.
Gloria in excelsis Deo, gloria in excelsis, gloria in ex-
Alto.
gloria in excelsis,
Tenore.
Gloria in excelsis Deo, gloria in excelsis, in ex-
Basso.
gloria in
Violoncello.
Basso.

a 2.
f
decresc.
p
cel - sis, glo-ri-a — in ex-cel - sis, — in ex-cel - sis De - o,
glo - ri-a,
cel - sis, glo-ri-a — in ex-cel - sis, — in ex-cel - sis De - o,
— ex-celsis,

a 2.
f
cresc.
te, glo - ri_fi_camus, glo - ri_fi - camus te, glorifi - camus te, glorifi - ca - - mus
glo - ri_fi_camus te,
te, te, glo - ri_fi - camus te, glorifi - camus te, glorifi - ca - - mus
glo_ri_fi_camus, glo - ri_fi - camus te,

cresc.
ff
a 2.
p
te, laudamus te, benedicimus te, glorificamus te. adoramus
te, laudamus te, benedicimus te, glorificamus te, adoramus

ff
p
pizz.
te!
Gra_tias a_gimus ti_bi prop_ter magnam gloriam tu -

p
p
am,
Do - mine De - us, Rex coe -
am,
am,
gra - tias a - gimus ti - bi prop - ter magnam glori - am tu - am,
arco
pizz.

le - stis, gra_ti_as a_gimus ti - bi,
gratias a_gimus ti - bi,
gra_ti_as a_gimus ti - bi,
De - us, Pa - ter om_ni - po - tens,
gratias a_gimus ti - bi,
arco

arco
arco
Do - - mi_ne Je - su Chri - ste, gra_ti_as a_gimus ti - bi,
gra_ti_as a_gimus ti - bi, Fi - -
pizz.

a 2.
arco
gra_ti_as a_gimus ti - bi.
li u - ni - ge - ni_te, gra_ti_as a_gimus ti - bi.
arco
arco

cresc.
ff
f
fz
Glo_ri_a in excelsis De_o,
glo_ri_a in ex_cel_sis,
glo_
Glo_ri_a in excelsis De_o,
glo_ri_a in ex_cel_sis,

glo-ri-a in ex-cel - sis, glori-a — in ex-cel-sis, — in ex-cel-sis De - o!
-ri-a in ex-celsis, glo - ri - a,
in ex-cel - sis, glori-a — in ex-cel-sis, — in ex-cel-sis De - o!
glo-ri-a in — ex-celsis,

cresc.
ff
a 2.
p
Lau - da - mus te, bene - di - cimus te, glo - ri - fi - ca - mus te, a - do - ramus, be - ne - di - cimus
Lau - da - mus te, bene - di - cimus te, glo - ri - fi - ca - mus te, a - do - ramus, be - ne - di - cimus

Andante con moto.
ff
decresc.
p
te,
glorifi - ca - mus, lau - da - mus te!

ff
fz
decresc.
p
pp
Domi_ne Deus, a_gnus Dei, qui tollis pecca_ta mundi, pecca_ta mundi,

a 2
a 2.
a 2.
mi_se_-re_re, mi_se_rere nobis, mi - se - re - re no - bis,
Domine Deus, a_gnus De_i,
mi_se_-re_re, mi_se_rere nobis, mi - se_rere no - bis,

decresc.
p
pp
decresc.
p
pp
decresc.
p
pp
decresc.
p
pp
decresc.
p
pp
decresc.
p
pp
mi - se - re - re, mi - se - re - re no - bis, mi - se -
decresc.
p
pp
qui tollis pecca - ta mundi, pecca - ta mundi,
decresc.
p
pp
mi - se - re - re, mi - se - re - re nobis,
mi - se -
decresc.
p
pp
decresc.
p
pp

a 2.
a 2.
pp
ff
fz
ffz
decresc.
p
f
re - re no - bis, Fi_li_us Patris, a_gnus De_i, qui tollis pecca _ ta mundi,
mi_se_rere no - bis,
re - re no - bis, Fi_li_us Patris, a_gnus De_i, qui tollis pecca _ ta mundi,

pp
a 2.
ff
f
pecca_ta mundi, mi_se_re_re, mi_se_re_re no_bis, mi_se_re_re no - bis,
mi_se_re_re, mi_se_re_re nobis, mi_se_re_re no - bis, Domine
pecca_ta mundi, mi_se_re_re

a 2.
ff
fz
Domine Deus, a_gnus De_i, Fi_li_us Patris, a_gnus De_i, qui tol_lis pec_ca_ta,
Deus, a_gnus De_i, Fi_li_us Patris, a_gnus Dei. qui tol_lis pec_ca_ta, pec_ca_ta

fff
dim.
p
pp
peccata mundi, miserere nobis!
mundi, miserere, miserere nobis!

Tempo I.
Quo_ni_am tu so_lus sanctus, quo - niam tu so_lus sanctus, quo - ni_am tu so_lus al_
quo - niam tu so_lus al - tis - simus,
Quo_ni_am tu so_lus sanctus, quo - niam tu so_lus sanctus, quo - ni_
quo - ni_am, quo_

cresc.
tis - simus, quo_niam ___ tu solus Dominus, ___ tu solus Do - - - mi_nus, tu so -
quo _ niam tu so _ lus, ___
am tu so _ lus, ___ tu solus Dominus, ___ tu solus Do - - - mi_nus, tu so -
niam tu solus al tis si mus,

lus, tu san ctus, al tis si mus, quoniam tu so_lus al tis si mus,
lus, tu san ctus, al tis si_mus, quoniam tu so_lus al tis si_mus,

Moderato.
quoniam tu so_lus Do_mi_nus!
quoniam tu so_lus Do_mi_nus!
Cum
Cum sancto Spi_ri_tu in glo_ri_a De_i_ Pa_tris, a_ _ _ men, cum sancto

a 2.
f
f
f
Cum sancto
sancto Spi - ri - tu in glo - ri - a De - i Pa - tris, a - - - - - - - - men, cum sancto Spiri -
Spi - ri - tu in glo - ri - a De - i Pa - tris, a - - men, a - - - - - - - - men, cum sancto

a 2.
f
f
f
Cum sancto Spi - ri-
Spi - ri - tu in glo - ri - a De - i Pa - tris, a - - - - - men, cum sancto Spi - ri - tu in glo -
tu in glo - - ri - a De - i Pa - tris, a - - men, a - - - - - men, cum sancto Spi - ri-
Spi - ri - tu, cum sancto Spi - ri - tu in glo - - ri - a De - i Patris, a - - men,

tu in glo - ri-a De - i Pa - tris, a - - - - - - - - - - - - men, cum sancto Spi-ri-
- ri-a De-i Pa - tris, a - - men, a - - - - - - - - - - - - men, a-
tu, cum sancto Spi-ri - tu in glo - - ri-a De - i Patris, a - - - - - - - - - men, cum sancto
cum sancto

tu in glo - ri_a De_i Pa_tris, cum san_cto Spi - ri_tu in
- - men, a - - - - men, cum san_cto Spi - ri - tu in glo - ri - a, in
Spi - ri - tu in glo_ri_a De_i Pa - tris, a - - - - - - men, cum san_cto
Spi - ri_tu in glo - - ri_a De - i Pa - tris, cum san_cto

a 2.
glo - - ri_a De - - i Pa - - tris, a - - men, a - - - - men, cum sancto
cum
Spi - ri - tu in glo - - ri_a De - - i Pa - - tris, a - - - men, cum

a 2.
Spi_ri_tu in glo_ _ ri_a De_i Pa_ _ tris, a _ men, a_men, a_ _
sancto Spi _ ri_tu in glo _ ri_a De_i_ Pa_tris, a _ _ _ _ men, a _ _ _ _ _
sancto Spi _ ri_tu, cum sancto Spi_ri _ tu in glo_ri_a De _ _ i Pa_tris,
cum san cto Spi _ ri_tu in glo _ _ ri _ a De_i

- men, a - men, a - men, a - men, a - men, a - men, a - men, a - men, a - men, a - men, a - men,
in glo - ri - a De - i Pa - tris, a - men, a - men, a - men, a - men, a - men, a - men, a - men.
Pa - tris, a - men, a - men, a - men, a - men, a - men, a - men, a - men, a -

a - men, a - - men,
a - - - men,
cum
a - men, a - - men,
cum sancto Spi - ri - tu in glo - - ri - a De - i - Pa - tris, cum sancto
- - - men, cum sancto Spi - ri - tu in glo - ri - a De - i - Pa - tris, a - - - - - men, cum

cum sancto Spi - ri - tu in glo - - ri - a De - - i Pa - tris,
sancto Spi - ri - tu in glo - - ri - a De - i Pa - - tris, a - men, a - - men,
Spi - ri - tu in glo - - ri - a De - i Pa - tris, a - - men, a - - men, cum
sancto Spi - ri - tu in glo - - ri - a De - i Pa - tris, a - men, a - men, a - - - men,

a 2.
a 2.
a - men, a - men, a - men, a - men, a - men, a - men, a - men, a - men, a - men, a -
san - cto Spi - ri - tu - in - glo - ri - a De - i Pa - tris, a - men, a - men, a - men,
a - men, a - men, a - men, a - men, a - men, a - men, a - men,

a 2.
men,
cum sancto Spi-ri-tu in glo-
men,
cum sancto Spi-ri-
cum sancto Spi-ri-tu in glo-ri-a De-i Pa-tris,
a-men, cum sancto Spi-ri-tu in glo-ri-a De-i Pa-tris, a-

ri_a De - - i_ Pa - - tris, a - men, a - - men, a_men, a_men, a - - men,
tu in glo - ri_a De_i_ Pa_tris, a - - men, a - - men, a_men, a_men, a - -
a - men, a - - men, a - - men, a_men, a_men, a - - men,
men, a_men, a_men, a - - men,

a - - men, a - - men. a - - - - men. a - men.
- - men, a - - men, a - - - - men, a - men,
a - men, a - - - - - - - men. a - men. a - men,
a - - men, a - - men, a - - men, a - men, a - men,

in glo-ri-a De-i Pa-tris
cum san-cto Spi-ri-tu in glo-ri-a De-i
cum san-cto Spi-ri-tu in glo- - ri-a
cum sancto Spi-ri-tu in glo- - ri-a De-i

a - men, a - men, a - - men, a - men, a - - men,
Pa - tris,
Patris, a - men, cum san - cto Spi - ri - tu in glo - ri - a De - - i, in glo - ri - a De - i
Pa - tris, a - - men, a - - mon, a - - men, a men, a - - men,
fz

a - men. a - men, a - - - men, a - - - - - - - - men!
Pa - tris, a - men, a - - men, a - - - - - - - - - men!
a - men, a - men, a - men, a men!

Credo.

Moderato.
Oboi.
Clarinetti in B.
Fagotti.
Corni in Es.
3 Tromboni.
Timpani in Es. B.
Violino I.
Violino II.
Viola.
Soprano.
Alto.
Tenore.
Basso.
Violoncello.
Basso.
p
pp
pizz.
Cre - - - do in unum De - - um,
Cre - - - do in unum De - - um,

pizz.
pp
pizz.
pp
pizz.
pp
p
p
p
pp
pp
fa - cto - rem coe-li et ter - rae, vi - si - bi - li-um om - ni-um et in -
fa - cto - rem coe-li et ter - rae, vi - si - bi - li-um om - ni-um et in -

arco
f
p
cresc.
vi-si-bi-li-um, et in-vi-si-bi-li-um.
vi-si-bi-li-um, et in-vi-si-bi-li-um.
Credo in

pizz.
pizz.
pizz.
Credo in unum Dominum Jesum Chri - - stum, cre-do in Fi-li-um De-i u-ni-ge-
Dominum Jesum Chri - - stum,
Credo in Jesum Chri - stum, cre-do in Fi-li-um De-i u-ni-ge-
unum Do - minum Je - sum Chri - - stum,
pizz.
pizz.

pizz.
arco
-ni-tum,
an-te omni-a sae- - cu-la,
De-um de De-
et ex Patre na-tum an-te omni-a sae-cu-la,
ni - tum,
et ex Patre na - tum,
De-um de De-
et ex Patre na-tum an-te om - ni-a sae- - cu-la,

p
o, lumen de lu - mi - ne, De-um ve - rum de De-o ve - ro,
o, lumen de lu - mi - ne, De-um ve - rum de De-o ve - ro,

f
f
f
arco
f
arco
f
arco
f
f
per quem om_ni_a, per quem om_ni_a fa - - - cta sunt,
f
per quem om_ni_a fa - - cta sunt.
f
per quem om_ni_a fa - cta sunt,
f
per quem om_ni_a fa - - cta sunt, per quem fa - - cta sunt, per quem om_ni_a
arco
f
arco
f

f
decresc.
p
p
p
per quem om-ni-a fa - cta sunt,
per quem om-ni-a fa - - cta sunt,
per quem om-ni-a fa - - - - - - - cta sunt,
fa - - cta om - ni-a fa - - cta sunt,
p
p

pizz.
pizz.
pizz.
p
qui propter nos ho-mi-nes et prop-ter nostram sa-lu-tem
p
p
qui propter nos ho-mi-nes et prop-ter nostram sa-lu-tem
p
pizz.
pizz.

decresc.
pp
decresc.
pp
p
p
p
pp
decresc.
pp
decresc.
pp
decresc.
pp
de - scen - dit, de - scen - dit de coe - lis.
de - scen - dit, de - scen - dit de coe - lis.
decresc.
pp
decresc.
pp

Andante.
Trombe in Es.
pp
pizz.
p
Ten. I. Solo
Et in_car_natusest de_

pp
pp
Spi - - ri_tu san_cto ex Ma_ri - - a, Mari_a vir_gi_ne, et homo fa - - ctus

pp
pp
est,
et incarna_tus est,
et incarna_tus est
deSpiritu
san_cto,
de
Ten. II. Solo
Et
in_car_na_tusest
de
Spi
ri_tu
san_cto
ex Ma_

pp
pp
Sopr. Solo
Et incar
Spi ri tu sancto ex Ma ri a vir gine, et ho mo fa ctus est.
ri a. Mari a vir gine, et homo fa ctus est, et incarnatus

pp
pp
pp
pp
natus est de Spi - - ri-tu san-cto ex Ma-ri - - a, Mari-a vir-gine, et
et in-carna-tus est de Spiritu san-cto ex Mari-a vir - gine, Mari-a vir-gine, et
est, et incarnatus est de Spiri-tu san-cto, de Spi-ritu sancto ex Ma-ri-a virgine,

decresc.
fp
p
decresc.
ppp
cresc.
Tutti pp
Tutti
homo fa - ctus est,
cru - ci-fi - xus e - ti-am pro no - bis sub
et ho-mo fa-ctus est,
arco

cresc.
f
pp
decresc.
ppp
Pon - ti - o Pi - la - to,
cru - ci -
cru - ci - fi - xus
3

cresc.
f
ff
fi _ xus e _ ti_am pro no _ bis sub Pon _ ti _ o Pi _ la _ to e _ ti_am cru _ ci _
e _ ti_am pro no _ bis sub Pon _ ti_o Pi_la _ to, sub Pon _ ti_o Pi_la _ to, cru _ ci _

fff
decresc.
pp
p
pizz.
fi - - - xus,
pas - sus et se - pul - - - tus
fi - - - xus,
pas - sus et se - pul - - - tus

est,
Solo
et in_car_na_tus est de
est,
Ten. II. Solo
et incar_na_tus
pizz.
pp
pizz.
pp
pp
pp
pp

pp
pp
pp
pp
Spi - - ri - tu san - cto ex Ma - ri - - a, Mari - a vir - gine, et homo fa - - ctus
Ten. I. Solo
ex Mari - a vir - gine, Mari - a vir - gine, et homo fa - ctus
est do Spiri - tu san - cto, de Spi - ritu sancto ex Ma - ri - a vir - gine, et homo factus

decresc.
fp
cresc.
f
p
ppp
Tutti
pp
est
cru - - ci-fi - xus e - ti-am pro no - bis sub Pon-ti-o Pi-la - - to,
est,
arco

pp
ppp
f
pp
ppp
f
pp
f
ppp
f
pp
f
pp decresc.
ppp
cresc.
f
pp decresc.
ppp
cresc.
f
pp decresc.
ppp
cresc.
f
ppp
cresc.
cru - - ci - fi - - xus e - ti - am pro
ppp
cresc.
ppp
cresc.
cru - - ci - fi - - xus e - ti - am pro no - - bis sub
ppp
cresc.
pp decresc.
ppp
cresc.
f
pp decresc.
ppp
cresc.
f

a 2.
cresc.
ff
no - bis sub Pon - ti - o Pi - la - to, sub Pon - ti - o Pi - la - to, cru - ci - fi - xus
Pon - ti - o Pi - la - to, sub Pon - ti - o Pi - la - to, cru - ci - fi - xus e - tiam pro no - bis,

ff
fff
pp
decresc.
p
pizz.
e - ti - am pro no - bis, cru - ci - fi - - - - xus, pas - sus et se - -
e - ti - am pro no - bis, cru - ci - fi - - - xus, pas - sus et se - -

pul - - - tus est.
pul - - - tus est.
arco

Tempo I.

a 2
p cresc.
Et resur_re_xit ter_ti_a di_e se_cundum scriptu _ ras,
Et resur _ re _ xit.
Et resur_re_xit se_cundum scriptu _ ras.
Et resur_re_xit ter_ti_a di_e se_cun _ dum scrip _ tu _ ras, et a_

cresc.
et a_scendit in coe_lum, se_det ad dex_teram Pa_tris, et i_te_rum ven_tu_rus est, ven_
et a_scendit in coe_lum, et i_te_rum ven_tu_rus est, ven_
et a_scendit in coe_lum, et i_te_rum ven_tu_rus est, ven_
scendit in coe_lum, se_det ad dex_te_ram Pa_tris, et i_te_rum ven_tu_rus est, ven_tu_rus est

ff
ff
ff
ff
ff
decresc.
p
p
p
turus est cum glo - ri - a, ju - di - ca - re vi - vos et mortu - os, cu - jus re - gni non e - rit
turus est cum glo - ri - a, ju - di - ca - re vi - vos et mortu - os, cu - jus re - gni non e - rit
cum glo - ri - a, judi - ca - re vi - vos et mortu - os,

p
pp
fi - nis, non e - rit fi - - nis.
Cre - do in Spi - ri - tum sanctum
fi - nis, non e - rit fi - - nis.
Cre - do in Spi - ri - tum sanctum
pizz.
pizz.

pizz.
pizz.
pizz.
Do - - mi - num,
et vi - vi - fi - can - tem, qui ex Patre Fili - o - que pro - ce - dit,
Do - mi - num,
et vi - vi - fi - can - tem, qui ex Patre Fili - o - que pro - ce - dit,

f
arco
qui cum Pa_tre et Fi_li_o simul a_do_ra - - - tur, qui lo_cu_tus
qui cum Pa_tre et Fi - li_o a_do_ra_tur,
qui con_glorifi - ca - tur,
qui cum Patre et Fi_li_o simul a_do_ratur et con_glo_ri_fi_ca - - tur, qui lo_cu_tus est per pro_

est — per pro - phe - - - tas. Con - fi - teor u - num bap - tis - ma in re - mis - si - o -
qui lo - cu - tus est per prophe - - tas.
qui lo - cu - tus est per prophe - tas. Con - fi - te - or u - num bap - tis - ma in re - mis - si - o -
phe - tas, per pro - phe - - - - tas.
pizz.

p
pp
arco
p
arco
p
arco
p
f
nem pecca_to_rem mor_tu _ o _ _ _ rum,
nem pecca_to_rem mor_tu _ o _ _ _ rum,
et vitam ven_tu_ri sae_cu_
arco
p
arco
p

a 2.
f
et vi_tam ven_tu _ ri sae_cu_
et vi_tam ven_tu_ri sae_cu_li, ven_tu_ri sae_culi, a_ _ _ _ _ men, a_
li, ven_tu_ri sae_culi, a _ _ men, ven_tu_ri sae_culi, a _ _ men, a _ _ men, a_

a 2.
f
et vi _ tam ven_tu _ ri sae_cu _ li, ven_tu _ ri_ sae_culi, a - men, a - - -
li, ven_tu_ri sae_culi, a - - - - men, ven_tu _ ri_ sae_cu_li, a - - - - men, a - - -
- - men, a - - - men, et vi_tam ven_tu _ ri sae_culi, a - men, a - - - - men, a - -
- - - men, et vi_tam ven_tu _ ri

men, a - - men, a - - - men, a - - - - - men, et vi_tam ven_tu_ri sae_cu_li, ven_
men, a - - men, a - - - - - - men, a - - men, a - - - - - - -
men, a - men, a - men, a - - - - - men, et vi_tam ven_tu_ri
sae_cu_li, ven_tu_ri_ sae_culi, a - - - - - - - men,

tu - ri_ sae - cu - li, a - - - - - - - - men, a - - - - - - - - - - men, a - -
men, a - - - - men, a - - - - men, et vi - tam ven - tu - ri sae - cu - li, a - -
sae - cu - li, a - - - - - - - - - - - - men,
et vi - tam ven - tu - ri sae - cu - li, a - men, a - - men,

men. a - - - - - - - men, a - - men, a - - - - - - men,
- men, a - - - - - - - - - - men, a - - - - - men, a - - men. a - - - men,
a - - - - - - - - - - - men, a - - - men, a - - men, a - - men,
a - - - - - - - - - - - - - - men, a - - - - - - - - men,

a - - - - - - - - - - men, a - men, a - men, a - - - - men,
a - - men, a - - - men, a - - - - - men, a - - - - - men,
a - - men, a - - - men, a - - - men, a - - - - - - men,
a - - - - - - - - - - - - - men, a - men, a - - men

a - men, a -
a - - - men, a - - men, a -
a - - - men,
et vi - tam ven - tu - ri sae - cu - li, ven - tu - ri - sae - cu - li. a - - - men, a -

men, a - - men, a - men, a - - men, a - - men, a - - men, a - men,
men, a - - men, a - - men, a - - men, a - - men, a - men, a -
a - - men, a - - men, a - men, a - men, a - - men, a - - men,
men, a - - men, a - - men, a - - mon, a - men, a - men, a - men.

a 2.
a_men, a - men, a - - - - - - - - men,
_men, a - - men, a - - - - - - - - men, et vi_tam ven_tu - ri sae_cu-
a_men, a - men, a - - - - - - - men, a - men, a - - - men, a-
a - men, a - men, et vi_tam ven_tu - ri sae_cu_li, ven_tu_ri_ sae_culi, a - - - men, a-

a 2.
f
et vi_tam ven_tu_ri sae_cu_li, ven_tu_ri sae_cu_li, a - - men, a_
li, ven_tu_ri_ sae_cu_li, a - - men, a_men, a_men, a_
- - - - men, a - - men, a - - - - men, et vi_tam ven_tu_ri sae_culi,
- men, a - - men, a - - men, a - - - - - - men, a men, a_

sae-cu-li, a - - - - - - men, a - - - - - men, a - - - - - - men,
- men, a - men, a - - men, a - - men, a - - - - men,
a - men, a - - men, a - - men, a - - men, a - - - - - men,
- - - - - men, a - - - - men, et vi-tam ven-tu-ri sae-cu-li, a - - men, et
trm

et vi _ tam ven _ tu _ ri sae_cu _ li, ven_tu _ ri sae_culi
et vi_tam ven _ tu _ ri sae_cu _ li, a _ _ men, et vi_tam ven_tu _ ri sae_cu_li, a _ _ _
vi_tam ven _ tu _ ri sae_cu _ li. ven_tu _ ι_ sae_cu _ li,
et vi _ tam ven_tu _ ri sae _ _

a - - men, a - - - - men,
et
a - - men, a - - - - men,
et
- men, a - - men, a - - - men,
- culi, a - - - men, a - - - men,
et vi -
p

vi_tam ven_tu _ ri sae_cu _ li, ven _ tu _ ri_ sae_cu _ li, et vi_tam ven_tu _ ri sae_cu _ li, ven_
et vi_tam ven_tu _ ri sae_cu _ li, a _ _ men, et_ vi _ tam ven_tu _ ri sae_culi,
tam ven _ tu _ ri sae_cu _ li, a _ _ _ men, et vi _ tam ven_tu _ ri sae _ cu _ li._
p

cresc.
f
tu_ri_ sae_culi, a _ men, et vi_tam ven_tu _ ri sae_cu _ li, et vi_tam ven_tu _ ri sae _ _ culi.
a _ _ _ _ _ _ men, et vi_tam ven_tu _ ri sae_cu _ li, et vi_tam ven_tu _ ri sae _ _
_venturi sae_culi, a_men, a _ _ _ _ _ _ _ _ _ _ _ _ _ _

a - - - men, a - - - - men, a - - - - - - men.
a - - - men, a - - - - - men, a - - - - - - men.
- cu-li, a - - men, a - - - - men, a - - - - - men.
- - men, a - - men, a - - - - - - men.

Sanctus.

Adagio.
Oboi.
Clarinetti in B.
Fagotti.
Corni in Es.
Trombe in Es.
3 Tromboni.
Timpani in Es.B.
Violino I
Violino II.
Viola.
Soprano.
Alto.
Tenore.
Basso.
Violoncello.
Basso.
San - ctus, san - ctus, san - - -
San - ctus, san - ctus, san - - -

p cresc.
fff
fz
ctus
Domi_nus De_us Sa_baoth!
Pleni sunt coeli, coe_li et ter_ra
Pleni sunt coeli glo_ri_a tu_a, coe_li et ter_ra
Pleni sunt coeli et ter _ ra, ple_ni sunt coeli, coe_li et ter_ra

gloria tu - a!
San - ctus,
san - ctus,
glori-a tu - a!
San - ctus,
san - ctus,

san - ctus
Domi-nus De-us Sa - baoth!
Ple-ni sunt coeli,
san - ctus
Domi-nus De-us Sa - baoth!
Ple-ni sunt coeli,
Pleni sunt coe-li et ter - ra,

Ple_ni sunt coeli, coe_li et ter_ra glo_ri_a tu_a,
pleni sunt coeli et terra gloria tu_
coe_li et terra, coe_li et ter_ra glo_ri_a tu_a,
coe_li et terra, coe_li et ter_ra glo_ri_a tu_a,
pleni sunt coeli et terra gloria tu_
ple_ni sunt coeli, coe_li et ter_ra_ glo_ri_a tu_a,

Allegro, ma non troppo.

o - san - - na in ex - cel - - sis, o - san - na in ex - cel - sis De - - o, o -
san - - na, o - san - - na in ex - cel - - sis, in ex - cel - sis De - - - - o,
na, o - san - - na in ex - cel - - sis, o - san - na in ex - cel - sis De - - - o, o - san -
cel - - - sis, o - san - na in ex - cel - sis De - - - o,

san - - na in ex - cel - sis De - - o, o - san - - - - - - na!
o - sań - na in ex - cel - sis De - - o, o - san - - - - - - na!
- - na in ex - cel - sis De - - o, o - san - - - - - - na!
o - san - na in ex - cel - sis De - - o, o - san - - - - - na!

Benedictus.

Andante.
Oboi.
Clarinetti in B.
Fagotti.
Corni in Es.
3 Tromboni.
Violino I.
Violino II.
Viola.
Soprano.
Alto.
Tenore.
Basso.
Violoncello.
Basso.
Solo
Be _ ne _ di _ ctus qui ve_nit in nomi_ne Domi_ni, be_
Solo
Solo
Be _ ne _ di _ ctus qui ve_nit in no_mine Domi_ni. be_
Solo
p
pp

p
- - ne - di - ctus qui ve-nit in nomi-ne Do - mi - - ni, qui ve - - nit in no - mi-ne
- - ne - di - ctus qui venit in nomine Do - mi - - ni, qui ve - - - nit in no - mine
be - ne - di - ctus qui venit in nomine Do - mi-ni, qui ve - - nit in no - mine

Domini, qui ve - nit in nomine Domi - ni,
Domini, qui ve - nit in nomine Domi - ni,
Domini, qui ve - nit in nomine Domi - ni,
Tutti
be - ne - di - ctus qui

fz
decresc.
p
Tutti
Solo
be - ne - di - ctus qui ve - nit, be - ne -
be - ne - di - ctus qui ve - nit in no - mi - ne Do - mi - ni, be - ne - di - ctus qui
be - ne - di - ctus qui ve - nit in no - mi - ne Domini, in no - mi - ne Do - mi - ni, be - ne -
ve - nit in no - mi - ne Do - mi - ni, qui ve - nit in no - mi - ne, no - mi - ne Do - mi - ni,

Tutti
dictus qui venit, benedictus qui venit in nomine Domini, bene-
Tutti
venit in nomine Domini, qui venit in nomine Domini, bene-
Tutti
dictus qui venit in nomine Domini, in nomine Domini, benedictus qui
Solo
benedictus qui venit in nomine Domini, in nomine Domini,

di _ ctus qui ve _ nit in no _ mine Do _ mi _ ni, qui ve _ nit in nomi_ne Do_mi _ ni,
di _ ctus qui ve _ nit in no _ mine Do _ mi _ ni, qui ve _ nit in nomi_ne Do_mi _ ni,
ve _ nit in no _ mine, no _ mine Do _ mi _ ni, qui ve _ nit in nomi_ne Do _ mi _ ni,
Tutti
p
be _ ne _ di _ ctus qui ve _ nit in no _ mine Do _ mi _ ni, in nomine Do _ mi _ ni,

p
cresc.
decresc.
p>
cresc.
Solo
be - ne - di - ctus qui
be - ne di - ctus qui
pp

ve_nit in no_mine Domi_ni, be _ ne_dictus qui ve _ nit in no _ mi_ne Do _ mi _ ni, qui
ve_nit in no_mine Domi_ni, be _ ne_dictus qui ve _ nit in no _ mi_ne Do _ mi _ ni, qui
ve_nit in no_mine Domi_ni, be _ ne_dictus qui ve _ nit in no _ mi_ne Do _ mi _ ni, qui
ve_nit in no_mine Domi_ni, be _ nedictus qui ve _ nit in no _ mi_ne Do _ mi_ni, qui

ve - nit in no - mine Domi - ni, qui ve - nit in no - mi - ne Do - mi - ni,
Do - mi - ni,
ve - - nit in - no - mine Do - mini, in no - mine Do - mi - ni,
ve - - nit in no - mine Domi - ni, in no - mi - ne Do - mi - ni,

Tutti
be - ne - di - ctus qui
Tutti
be - ne - di - ctus qui ve - nit in no - mine
Tutti
be - ne - di - ctus qui ve - nit in no - mine Domi - ni, in no - mi - ne
Tutti
be - ne - di - ctus qui ve - nit in no - mi - ne Do - mi - ni, qui venit in no - mi - ne, in no - mine

decresc.
p
Solo
ve - nit, be - ne - di - ctus qui ve - nit in no - mi - ne Do - mi - ni, in no - mine
Do - mi - ni, be - ne - di - ctus qui ve - nit, qui ve - nit in no - mi - ne Do - mi - ni, in no - mine
Do - mi - ni, be - ne - di - ctus qui ve - nit in no - mi - ne Do - mi - ni, in no - mine
Do - mi - ni, be - ne - di - ctus qui ve - nit in no - mi - ne Do - mi - ni, in

p
p
p
p
p
p
p
p
p
Tutti
Do - mi - ni, be - ne - di - ctus qui ve - nit in no - mi - ne Do - mi - ni, qui ve -
Tutti
Do - - mi - ni, be - ne - di - ctus qui ve - nit in no - mi - ne Do - - mi - ni, qui ve -
Tutti
Do - - mi - ni, be - ne - di - ctus qui ve - nit in no - mine Domi - ni, in no - mine Domi - ni, qui ve -
Tutti
no - mine Do - mi - ni, be - - ne - di - ctus qui ve - nit in no - mi - ne Do - mi -

Allegro ma non troppo.
nit in no_mi_ne Do _ mi _ ni.
nit in no_mine Do_mi _ ni.
nit in no_mine Do _ mi _ ni.
O san_
ni, in no_mine Do _ _ mi _ ni.
Osanna, dal segno

Agnus Dei.

Andante con moto.
Oboi.
Clarinetti in B.
Fagotti.
Corni in Es.
Trombe in C.
3 Tromboni.
Timpani in C.G.
Violino I.
Violino II.
Viola.
Soprano.
Alto.
A - gnus De - i, qui
Tenore.
A - gnus De - i, qui tol - lis pec - ca - ta
Basso.
A - gnus De - i, qui tol - lis pec - ca - ta, pec - ca -
Violoncello.
Basso.

a 2.
A - gnus De - i qui tol - lis pec - ca - - - ta, pec - ca -
tol - lis pec - ca - - - ta mun - di, pec - ca -
mun - di, a - gnus De - - i, qui tol - lis pec -
- ta mun - di, a - gnus De - - i, qui tol - - lis pec - ca -

ta mun - - di, mi - se - re - re, mi - se - re - re no - - - bis,
ta mun - - di, mi - se - re - - re no - - - bis,
ca - ta mun - - di, mi - se - re - - - re no - - - bis
ta mun - - di, mi - se - re - - - - re no - - - bis,

a 2.
a 2.
a 2.
a - - gnus De - - i, qui tol - -
a - - gnus De - - i, qui tol - lis pec - ca - ta, pec - ca - - ta
a - - - - - gnus De - i, qui tol - lis pec - ca - ta mun - di,
a - -

lis pec - ca - - - - ta mun - di, pec - ca - ta mun -
mun - di, a - gnus De - - i, qui tol - lis pec - ca - ta, pec - ca - ta mun -
a - - gnus De - - i, qui tol - lis pec - ca - ta mun -
gnus De - i, qui tol - lis pec - ca - - - ta, pec - ca - ta mun -

p
fz
f
- di, —
mi - se - re - re no - bis,
- di, —
mi - se - re - re no - bis,
- di, —
mi - se - re - re no - bis,
- di, — mi - se - re - re, mi - se - re - re no - bis, a - gnus

a - - gnus De - - i, a -
a - - gnus De - - i, a - - gnus De - - i, qui tol -
a - - - - gnus De - - i, a - - gnus De - - i,
De - - i, qui tol - - lis pec - ca - - ta mun - - di, a - - gnus

a 2.
gnus De - i, qui tol - lis pec - ca - ta mun - di,
- lis pec - ca - ta, pec - ca - ta mun - di, a - gnus De - i, qui
qui tol - lis pec - ca - ta mun - di,
De - i, qui tol - lis pec - ca - ta mun - di, a - gnus

Andante.
in Es.
in Es. B.
a - gnus De - i, qui tol - lis pec - ca - ta mun - - di. Do - na no - bis
tol - lis pec - ca - ta, pec - ca - - ta mun - - di.
a - - gnus De - i, qui tol - lis pec - ca - ta mun - di. Do - na no - bis
De - - i, qui tol - lis pec - ca - - ta mun - - di.

p
p
p
p
pa - cem,
do - na
no - bis
pa - - cem,
pa - - cem,
do - na
no - bis
pa - - cem,

do - na no - bis pa - - cem, do - - na, do - na no - bis pa - -
do - na no - bis pa - - cem, do - - na, do - na no - bis pa -

p
cem,
do_na no - bis,
no_bis pa - cem,
cem,
do_na no - bis,
no_bis pa - cem.

pa - cem,
do - na, do_na no_bis
pa - cem,
do - na, do_na no_bis
do_na, do_na no_bis pa_cem, do_na no - bis pa_cem,

p
p
pp
pp
pp
Solo
p
pa - cem, pa - cem, pa - cem,
do - na,
Solo
p
do - na, do_na no_bis,
Solo
p
pa - cem, pa - cem, pa - cem,
do - na, do_na no_bis.
Solo
p
do - na, do_na no_bis pa - cem,
p
p

decresc.
decresc.
decresc.
do_na no_bis pa - cem, do_na no_bis pa - cem, do - na, do_na no_bis
do - - na pa - cem, do_na no_bis pa - cem, do - na, do_na no_bis, do - - na
do - - na pa - cem, do_na no_bis pa - cem, do - na, do_na no_bis, do - - na
do_na, do_na no_bis pa - cem, do - - na
decresc.
decresc.

pa - cem, do-na no-bis pa - cem, pa - cem, pa - cem,
do-na no-bis
pa - cem. do-na no-bis pa - cem, pa - cem, pa - cem,

decresc.
Tutti
Solo
do_na no_bis, no_bis pa - cem, do_na, do_na no_bis pa - - cem, do - na
pa - cem, do_na, do_na no_bis pa - cem,
do_na no_bis, do_na, do_na no_bis pa - cem, do_na, do_na no_bis pa - - cem, do - na
Soio
do_na no_bis pa - cem, do - na no_bis, do_na no_bis pa - - cem, do - na

Tutti
Solo
Tutti
no - bis pa - - cem, do - na no - bis pa - - cem,
do - na no-bis pa - cem, do - na
no - bis pa - - cem, do - na no - bis pa - - cem,
do - na no-bis pa - cem, do - na

Solo
Tutti
Solo
do na no bis pa - cem, do - na, do na no bis
no bis pa - cem, do - na no bis pa - cem,
do na no bis pa - cem, do - na, do na no bis
no bis pa - cem, do - na no bis pa - cem,

cresc.
Tutti
pa - cem, no-bis pa-cem, do-na no-bis pa - cem, pa -
do-na
pa - cem, do - na pa -
pa - cem, no-bis pa-cem, do-na no-bis pa - cem, pa -
pa - cem.

Allegro molto moderato.

ff
fz
decresc.
De - i, qui tol - lis pec - ca - ta, a - gnus De - i, a - gnus De - i,
ca - ta mun - di,
a - gnus De - i, a - gnus De - i, a - gnus De - i,
a - gnus De - i qui tol - lis pec - ca - ta,

Andantino.
pp
a 2.
cresc.
f
p
do_na no_bis pa - cem, do_na no_bis pa - cem, do_na no_bis pa_cem, do - na
do_na no_bis — pa_cem, do_na no_bis pa - cem, do_na no_bis pa_cem, do - na